ID0604841

RUSSIA

A CROSSROADS BETWEEN HISTORY AND NATURE

WHITE STAR PUBLISHERS

Text
Arnaldo Alberti

Graphic design
Anna Galliani

Map
Arabella Lazzarin

Translation
Antony Shugaar and Ann Ghiringhelli

Contents

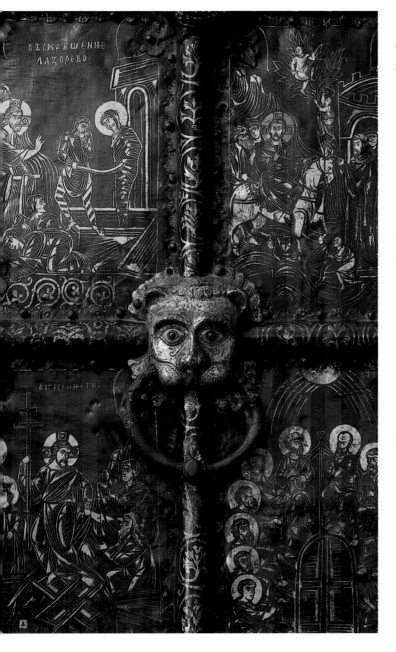

1 *The photographer's lens settled on a detail by Vassily Blazhennif on the gorgeous bulb-shaped domes, a colorful and precious symbol of Russia's long, glorious, and tumultuous history.*

2-3 *The true Russian name of Red Square is Krasnaya Ploshchad' – krasnaya meaning "beautiful," which is linked to the concept of "red" only because red is beautiful. In this view of the northeast side, the building of the State Historical Museum is visible.*

4-5 *Arriving in the Kamchatka Peninsula, on the far edge of Siberia, is not unlike landing on the moon. Even when viewed from the comfort of a plane, its arid landmass, with scattered lakes and craters, holds a strange and intimidating fascination. The peninsula has no fewer than 28 still active volcanoes, all over 9850 ft high. And yet Kamchatka is also a productive region, supplying most of the bricks needed by Siberia's building industry and the best fish in the Pacific Ocean.*

6-7 *Lake Kronos is on the western side of the huge inactive volcano of the same name which towers 11.575 ft above it. It is situated immediately over the caldera, and the heat rising from the depths of the volcano makes its waters permanently blue. The lake looks like an enormous precious stone set against the mountainside which, by contrast, is perpetually covered by ice and snow.*

8 *The Golden Gates (1158-1164) of the fortified town of Vladimir, embellished with engravings depicting episodes from the Gospels, were extensively restored several times during the 17th and 18th centuries to*

eliminate wear and tear caused more by vandalism than by age. They have thus reached the 20th century in an excellent state of conservation and UNESCO has included them among the works considered to form the world's most precious artistic heritage.

9 *Among the many towers and domes of the cathedrals within the Moscow Kremlin, the bell tower of Ivan III (the Great) is surely the most splendid. Designed by Bon Fryazin, an architect of Italian origin, work started on it in 1505 and was completed in the space of three years. With its gilded cupola it points heavenwards, a distinctive feature within the harmonious framework of the Kremlin's churches.*

12-13 *This picture shows the interior of the Moscow's Bolshoi Theater (the "Big" Theater) and it is certainly one of the greatest worldwide. Not only on account of its undeniably imposing dimensions, but also for the exceptional level of its productions and performers for over a century.*

14-15 *A little Muscovite has his picture taken in front of the Bolshoi Theater. Its Neoclassical façade and impressive size make this building a point of reference in the urban landscape of the Russian capital.*

16-17 *The oldest church in the complex is that of the Holy Trinity, rebuilt in 1422 on the site where the original wooden church built by St. Sergius stood. The bell-tower, in Rococo style, on the side of the Cathedral of the Assumption, is the work of D.V. Ukhtomsky and rises 289 ft. All around, there are other gorgeous churches (St. Peter, of Our Savior, Sts. Zosima and Savvati, and St. Sergio), the refectory, and the house of the archbishop.*

18-19 *The Moscow River flows slowly in the last hours of dusk, caressing elegant palaces and majestic bridges. The city's earliest nucleus developed along the banks of this river. Today Moscow is a boundless metropolis.*

© 2006 White Star S.p.A.
New updated edition

© 1995 White Star S.p.A.
Via Candido Sassone, 22/24
13100 Vercelli, Italy - www.whitestar.it

ISBN 88-544-0070-X

Reprints:
    3 4 5 6   10 09 08 07 06

Printed in Singapore

Introduction

There is a Russia you can see, with its breathtaking
landscapes, cities, villages, peoples, forests and ancient
treasures. There is another Russia that you can't see,
no less enchanting, hidden and tucked away inside
the visible Russia. The traveler desires always to have
that invisible Russia unveiled and described, so that
he can enjoy, during his voyage, a complete
appreciation, understanding, and enjoyment of both
Russias, together, as a physical and spiritual whole.

The czars, lest we forget, were emperors of Russia
and more, considering that – and still today – more
than one of them exists in a geographical-political
sense: Great Russia (that of Moscow and St.
Petersburg), Uralic Russia, Siberian Russia, and that
of the Far East, never forgetting, however, that
Belarus is still White Russia, as Ukraine or Malorussia
is Little Russia. Truly Russia is, in its sociocultural
magnitude, so manifold that the shrewd visitor can
physically and perfectly appreciate, understand, study,
and visit the same itineraries, places, and physical and
temporal spaces of this immense country, each time
with different and highly diversified spiritual and
intellectual experiences. Thus, present-day Russia can
be encountered, full of new stimuli and determined in
its emulation of the more advanced countries of the
West, characterized, consequently, by a great craving
– almost an obsession – for modernization. This is a
Russia that clearly demonstrates its eagerness to
quickly fill the technological gap that has widened
over the past and to offer – thanks to newfound
entrepreneurial freedom – enticing investment
opportunities for foreign capital. In this case, we are
passing through the very latest Russia, the disciple of
the West, straining powerfully to grasp the prophecy
of the liberal-consumer miracle economies of the
West, with a natural wealth of incalculable resources
and natural wonders, already marked by an industrial
architecture all its own, with a nicely developed neo-
capitalistic spirit, and by a landscape increasingly
dotted and overgrown with new industrial plants and
factories with the emblems of multinational
corporations, research centers, and trading offices,
with plaques more often than not an American
trademark transcribed into Cyrillic-script.

The visitor, who may happen to be free of any
weighty or immediate concerns, can also stroll
through the streets of many other Russias: for
instance, there is a Russia of unique landscapes,
including those of the gruelling, endless, exceedingly
varied monotony of the steppe, with its "light-blue
that drags at the eyes, of which one can see neither

beginning nor end." This is the scene that is offered to the eyes through the endless forests, the forests standing alongside god-forsaken villages, as well as the brightly colored provincial towns, and even the two densely populated metropolises of Russia, landscapes that sooner or later redeem their apparent uniformity with unexpected visions of authentic architectural masterpieces.

For example, a traveler that decides to tour the circuit of historical towns that make up the "Golden Ring" will see a myriad of fortified citadels (kremlins), with massive towers, donjons, and keeps, as well as the glittering, scintillating silvery or golden onion domes of churches and cathedrals within.
These kremlins have the power to transform the traveler on the spot into an astonished spectator, set at center-stage on that vast, vivid, and rich theater that is the Russian plain, opening its ancient gates to the visitor, inviting him or her to enter, offering the never-ending miracle of renewal, always fresh and new, solemn and magnificent, in its millennium-old rituals. The liturgical rituals are accompanied by music and song, which can only be described as sublime. The thunderstruck spectator remains for long minutes unable to distinguish heaven from earth. But behind the procession of saints, on the fields "sounds the happy noise of dancing," and suddenly the scenery changes and the stage is thronged with dancers giving their all, almost orgiastically, followed by songs of love and of joy, and then there are choruses of women intoning chants of heart-rending sadness – and all this magic material belongs to the heritage of Slavic and Russian folklore.

With this music ringing in his heart more than in his ears, our traveler can continue on his way with confidence through the streets of the cities and towns, where sidewalks, shopwindows, and museums will reveal and unfold, in a permanent exhibition, the true masterpieces of craftsmanship, with the solid and colorful beauty of finely carved wooden objects, alternating with the exceedingly refined vestments and embroidered draperies of tradition, and the skillful creations of the goldsmith.

Russia also means Asia, and certainly not in the sense that we Occidentals have so lazily attributed to the term. Suffice it to point out, perhaps, that the Greeks described Asia as only a small plot of land, really, inhabited by the Alani, an ancient people, and beginning with the River Volga, running westward as far as the region north of the Caucasus. Arnold Toynbee was right to find slightly ridiculous the 1312 ft high barrier (about 1300 ft, on average) of the Urals, which imprudent geographers designate as the boundary between Europe and Asia. This mountain chain is truly unconvincing, one is forced to agree, even as a mere local boundary between two provinces. This is a geographic line that does not even separate Siberia and European Russia, which instead continues undaunted eastward, with the same peoples, the same

20 *Red Square stretches along the eastern walls of the Kremlin, bordered to the south by the Cathedral of the Intercession, to the north by the History Museum and the Ascension Gates, and to the east by the Our Lady of Kazan Cathedral and the GUM department store with its upper-level galleries. GUM stands for "Gosudarstvenny Universalny Magazin." Counters of every kind proliferate everywhere, in tribute to now widespread western-style consumerism.*

21 *Hard Rock Café on Arbat Street, in the capital, is a symbol of Russia's new direction. The products and lifestyle that once stood for anti-Sovietism and were considered subversive are today part of Muscovites' daily life. It is no accident that the second language spoken by young Russians today is English: they look to the Anglo-Saxon world, and particularly America, when thinking of models for their own future.*

landscape, the same harsh climate. To see Russia means, therefore, seeing at the same time, and with no distinction, Europe and Asia joined as one; it means traveling through Eurasia, which is actually a more solid and concrete continent than many scholars seem to have hitherto understood. Perhaps it is no accident that there is such a dizzying and unpredictable round-robin of explanations that have been offered concerning the origins of the name "Russia," with hypotheses that range from the name of a small town not far from Kiev, and other, far more intricate derivations from Finno-Ugaric. It is not to overvalue it, but simply because there is no metal considered to be more precious, that historian and art critics call the corona – the "Golden Ring" – of ancient cities that are around Moscow. Someone may remind the traveler that his ideal voyage through history ought to begin with the Rus' of Kiev. But Kiev is today the capital of the Independent Republic of the Ukraine. In fact, a Little Russia has seceded. In reality, of course, this happened nearly a thousand years ago. After the break-up, and we are talking about the 11th century here, of Great Kiev into many smaller principalities, comes the formation, farther north, of new, rich, and powerful trading cities.

First in the sequence was Vladimir, a town set in the center of a wooded region in the principality of Suzdal-Novgorod; Vladimir's power and importance grew after the prince Andrei Bogolyubov of Kiev, perhaps around 1160, transferred the precious and universally admired "Icon of the Mother of God" to Vladimir. The icon was known from then on as Vladimirskaya, and was considered always to be the celestial "Protectress of All the Russias." In fact, as early as 1169, Vladimir became the capital city of the principality and the see of the metropolitan. This marked the beginning of an era of much construction of churches, the fruit of the devotion of princes and merchants, beginning in 1158 with the building of an impressive cathedral dedicated to the Dormition of the Virgin Mary. This building, which has an unusual radial plan, surrounded by four upthrusting domes on the sides, and with a harmonious central dome, presents on the interior the image of an all-powerful Christus Pantocrator. Thereafter (between 1194 and 1197), at the orders of the grand duke of the city, Vsevolod III, another, equally important cathedral was built, and was dedicated to Dmitri. This cathedral, which was far less liturgical than many others, on its exterior has very little space devoted to religious pictorial art, featuring instead an abundant iconography consisting of depictions of animals, plants, and folk characters taken directly from the Russian oral tradition.

At Vladimir, particularly worthy of note is the Golden Door, dating from 1163, set above the Church of the Deposition of the Sacred Vestment, whose present-day overall appearance is the result of a painstaking and time-consuming restoration, that began after the Mongols were finally driven out, and which was completed only at the beginning of the 19th century. This Gate has the particular distinction of being the only Gate to survive the attacks of the Turkic-Mongol hordes, which invaded the country, beginning in 1230, destroying the elegant and stout Kremlins, the churches and the cathedrals, the palaces and monasteries, until not a stone remained standing, devastating, village by village, the luminous land of Russia.

Turning from Vladimir to Suzdal, running along the banks of the river Nerl, and thus running around the Golden Ring, at Kideska we come to the ruins of a great fortified castle dating from the 12th century, inside of which is preserved the most ancient stone church in all of northern Russia. Here, according to a reliable legend, the venerated martyr-brothers Boris and Gleb halted on their voyage back from Rostov to their native Kiev.

Also along the Nerl river, in the quiet of the verdant village of Bogolyubov, is that spiritual oasis, the elegant Church of the Protection of the Virgin Mary, built by Prince Andrei. Along this route one can also reach Suzdal, once the capital of the principality of Rostov-Suzdal, destroyed by the Tatar-Mongols, and rebuilt in the 13th century, and reinforced with a system of fortified monasteries. Of these, the Monastery of the Protection of the Virgin Mary survives almost completely intact, dating from 1364. In it, one can admire the churches of St. Lazarus, 1667, and of St. Antipius, dating from 1745, with its distinctive octagonal bell tower, which served as a winter church. The stupendous Kremlin contains within it the Cathedral of the Nativity of the Virgin Mary, glittering with icons and frescoes, recently restored to their original splendor. Certainly our description cannot equal the task of portraying the enchanting beauty of the Golden Doors, which can safely be called a true masterpiece of the icon-making art of ancient Russia. Equally wealthy in objects and paintings is the Monastery of the Savior and of St. Euthymius, once a prison, now an exquisite museum. The Bishop's Palace, a great outdoor museum of wooden architecture (it contains a detailed and painstaking reconstruction of an ancient Russian village), and the Monastery of Pokrovsky, one of the earliest surviving stone buildings, stand as reminders that the kremlins were originally all built entirely of wood. Suzdal, which has long been absent from the annals of wealth and power of Russian history, is nonetheless entirely visible in terms of artistic beauty, but it is also the invisible and imperishable heart of a third Russia, the Russia of the soul, which is the source of the aesthetic and moral grandeur of the Russians.

Older than Suzdal is Yaroslavl, founded in 1010 as a fortress, it played an important role in trade, by virtue of its location on Mother Volga, the mighty river that serves as a main communications artery through Russia. Material wealth and the abundance of

22 top *A young Muscovite poses sitting on the rim of a fountain, near which she has found some cool respite from the heat. The Russian summer can be as torrid as that of Western Europe.*

22 bottom *A white tulle dress, a bouquet of fresh flowers, and a wide smile on her face, this bride crosses the streets of Moscow after her wedding ceremony. There is much of the new Russia in this image, combining beauty, faith in the future, and desire to be noticed.*

gold never caused Yaroslavl to forget the wealth of the spirit, and thus the city succeeded in developing its own rich school of artistic production. One distinctive characteristic of Yaroslavl's art is the use of polychrome enamels and majolicas on the exteriors of buildings, such as those that cover the Church of the Epiphany of Christ, in the Monastery of the Transfiguration, dating from the 13th century, and the Church of the Prophet Elijah, dating from the 17th century.

The Golden Ring continues, with a slightly less exalted state of mind, perhaps, all the way to that shrine of eternal beauty, the city of Rostov the Great (Rostov Velikie), with its powerful and elegant towers, with its Kremlin that seems to have been created by the artistic brushstrokes of an imaginative stage artist, adorned with churches (such as the Church of the Resurrection of Christ), which contain paintings of indescribable beauty and an iconostasis which may be the most beautiful one on Earth. Rostov Velikij enjoyed its greatest political strength and artistic excellence during the 13th century. Defeated by Moscow, it lost economic standing, just as Suzdal had, but it maintained its artistic and religious stature (in the Russian Orthodox church, the two are inseparable, because it will be – according to the prophecy of Dostoevsky – beauty that will save the world, and they continue to grow and flourish the more that humans return to the values of the spirit).

The Golden Ring runs very close to Moscow where it passes through ancient Zagorsk, today Sergiev Posad, the headquarters of the Russian orthodoxy. It was founded as a monastery by St. Sergei of Radonez, who was converted to the monastic life after a number of years as a hermit. Upon the first wooden church that stood here now stands the elegant Cathedral of the Holy Trinity, for which Andrei Rublev painted the icon of the Holy Trinity, an unrivalled masterpiece of art and of theological intensity. One should not leave Sergiev without allowing one's eyes to gaze upon the vision of the gold and turquoise domes of the Church of the Holy Ghost, a vision that may accompany one forever.

Heading West, one comes to the mighty Novgorod, the first ancient river-trading town, where the Russians waited to trade with the Varangian merchants, men from the North who sailed down to purchase the manufactured goods and clothing that the Russians were willing to sell them. Novgorod was founded on the River Volchov in A.D. 862 by a Varangian, Rurik, who was fated to become the town's first prince. With Vladimir II the Great, the city of Novgorod converted en masse to Christianity, and as early as A.D. 1030, it was an episcopal see, and indeed even today the metropolitan bishop of Novgorod enjoys the same status as the metropolitan of St. Petersburg. The Kremlin of Novgorod, rebuilt in bricks at the end of the 15th century, is one of those that boasts the distinction of never falling to the

23 Immaculate flowerbeds, repainted historic palaces, and rooftop satellite antennas, men and women relaxing on benches after work: even these images, which could be from any European capital, demonstrate how the lifestyle in modern-day Moscow has changed with respect to the not-so-distant past.

24-25 On the fringes of the desolate tundra zone, the area at the foot of Mt. Kronos, one of 200 volcanoes in the Kamchatka peninsula, is actually a nature reserve. In spring and autumn its many plants and trees add further patches of color to this already verdant region, offering alternating harmony and contrast with the bleak, red earth of the surrounding peninsula.

Turkic-Mongol armies during their raids. On the contrary, the Golden Horde used its friendly relations with Novgorod to extend its commercial trade with the rest of Europe. The imposing cathedral of St. Sophia, built between 1045 and 1050, is intended to rival in proportion, form, and beauty its celebrated counterpart in Kiev.

Farther north, nothing remains of the ancient monastery of Anthony (possibly founded by a pious Catholic monk who had converted to the Russian Orthodox faith), except the cathedral of the Nativity of the Mother of God (1117). Among the treasures contained in the Museum of History, Architecture, and Art of Novgorod, even the least art-loving visitor will never be able to forget the great icon called the "Battle of the Novgorod against the Suzdal," dating from the middle of the 15th century. In the three scenes depicted in this icon, one can see Novgorod being besieged by the army of Suzdal, which seems about to swarm over the city walls, and then saved by the intercession of the Madonna, one of the most venerated icons in Russia.

From Novgorod, the Golden Ring continues through Pskov. To the ancient Russians, reaching Pskov meant completing the pilgrimage for knowledge and love of history and the spirit of the Russias, and succeeding finally in "glimpsing the summit of the Holy Trinity, source of all life."

The Kremlin of Pskov and the glittering domes of its churches, once visible from a very great distance, continue to shed the invisible light of a continuing inner spirituality that has preserved its message of faith and love, brought here also by Princess Olga of Kiev, who converted to Christianity and then preached the Gospel at Pskov and erected a cross there. In 1347, Pskov became independent from Novgorod and it built a spectacular cathedral dedicated to Holy Trinity, with impressive doors, which are certainly some of the loveliest in the world. The Cathedral of the Transfiguration of the Savior in the monastery of Miros is believed to be the oldest surviving stone structure in Pskov, and is certainly one of the oldest churches in Russia.

Although it is located outside of this historical circuit, one cannot fail to mention the wooden architectural complex of the island of Kizi, in the center of the Lake Onega, to the north of St. Petersburg. Then there were carved churches with a great number of bell towers covered with wooden roofing tiles (the Church of the Transfiguration, dating from 1714, has no fewer than twenty-two) and the interiors adorned with exquisite icons, which impress themselves in the memory of the fortunate visitor.

St. Petersburg, on the River Neva, where it flows into the Gulf of Finland, was built at the behest of the Czar Peter the Great, as a "window on Europe," as an example of the modernization of the country, and to deprive Moscow of its privileged position as the motor and heart of Russia. It was an invitation and a

summoning of the most respected and renowned architects, artists, and craftsmen of Europe, who competed to build new mansions and palaces in the style of 18th-century Europe on the shores of the Baltic Sea. Italians, including Quarenghi, Rastrelli, and Rossi, were invited to work there and the imprint of the Italian Renaissance can be seen clearly throughout the great historical heart of St. Petersburg and in the sumptuous summer palaces of the czars. The city quickly became exactly what it was meant to be: the scientific and cultural heart of the Russian Empire, with its more than forty schools, hundreds of institutes of scientific research, eighteen major theaters, and fifty museums, including the Hermitage, one of the most important in the world, and the more than two thousand public libraries, a major shipyard – one of the largest in Europe – the many large factories, and of course, the tourist attractions and many monuments to scientists, writers, musicians, generals, and czars. There are also the palaces and buildings in many different styles, ranging from the Baroque to the Oriental. There are the churches, monasteries and the bridges over the canals. It is a city that should be admired for its white nights and for the surreal atmosphere of its streets, especially the Nevsky Prospect, about which Gogol and Dostoevsky wrote so many remarkable pages, and upon which in part the myth of St. Petersburg is based.

The city begins with the Peter and Paul Fortress. Seen from the bank of the Neva, it does not seem all that massive or impressive, but as one gets closer to it one can see that it occupies most of the islet, with its six corner structures, sharply delineated hexagonal structures, elongated into bastions joined by straight parallel walls, the outermost of which is between four and 13 and 20 ft thick, while the innermost wall is between 3.5 and 5 ft thick. They range in height from 30 and 40 feet. This fortress, by a twist of fate, had as its most important involuntary guest the son of the builder, the czarevich Alexei, who was put to death there by his father Peter I. Among its most illustrious inmates were, unfortunately, many writers, beginning with Alexander Radischev, a renowned thinker and the author of A Journey from St. Petersburg to Moscow (1790, a travel journal that was also an indignant denunciation of the horrible conditions in which the serfs lived under Catherine II). In 1825, the Peter and Paul Fortress filled with Decembrists, who were largely revolutionaries of the upper classes, who rose in a revolt against the absolute power of the czar. In 1849, Fyodor Dostoevsky was imprisoned here, accused of conspiracy, and later the thinker and author Nikolai Chernyshevsky was locked up here. Here too in 1877 Alexander Ulyanov was condemned to death, opening a long series of events that ultimately led to Bolshevism, in as much as he was the brother of Vladimir Ilych Ulyanov – later named Lenin. In its interior, the fortress contains the handsome cathedral of Sts. Peter and Paul, in an elegant early Baroque style, the work of the Italian architect Domenico Trezzini. The gilded spire, rising 120 ft into the air, can be seen very clearly from the far side of the Neva, and for many years, its bell tower, 400 ft feet in height, was the tallest structure in Russia.

The church has an original iconostasis made of carved and gilded wood. Alongside the fortress stands the Cabin, the house that Peter the Great had built in only three days as a haven.

One crosses the Neva and, on the right, one finds the island of Vasilevski Island with its straight and orderly roads. Turning to the left, on the other hand, one encounters the vast palatial range of the Admiralty, which extends where there was once a dense forest of pine and birch trees, partly cut down in later years to allow for a road that ran straight to Moscow. Beginning in 1783, this road slowly became crowded with houses and every sort business: thus the Nevsky Prospect grew apace. The harmony of the entire development of the road is remarkable; in two hundred years, hundreds and hundreds of buildings had sprung up, side by side, houses and palaces, each of them different, but all of them compatible with one another, all of them the appropriate height to fit in with the road. At first, pedestrians paraded along a pine surface; but the increase in the number and weight of the passing vehicles made it necessary to lay down an asphalt surface.

The Nevsky Prospect is now the highway of business and commerce, but also of cultural institutes, restaurants, theaters, libraries, and cinema. Every building and every residence along Nevsky Prospect has an interesting history, all of them coming to an end in Nevsky Square, along the road that leads to Moscow, and at the gates of the Trinity monastery, which boasts two magnificent cathedrals. Let us set out again from the River Neva, in line with the Admiralty, and continue past the garden that ends in the majestic and impressive Cathedral of St. Isaac, which can accommodate 14,000 people. All of the statistics concerning this church are astonishing: from the 24,000 piles that make up the foundations, to the 112 columns weighing 130 tons each, 50 ft tall, the 382 sculptures, and the Foucault's pendulum dangling 321 ft. Continuing along the left bank of the Neva, one encounters the monument to Peter the Great, dedicated to him by Catherine II, and known as the "Bronze Horseman," from the poem by Pushkin. On the left side of the garden opens out the immense square of the Winter Palace, today incorporating the Hermitage Museum, overlooking which are the buildings of the Chiefs of Staff of the Military, the Ministry of Foreign Affairs, as well as the Arch of Triumph which leads to the Herzen Road, and then on to the Nevsky Prospect, just a few steps away from the museum (formerly the apartment) of Aleksander Pushkin. In the square stands a column (dedicated to the Czar Alexander I) in the finest tradition of the great squares of Italy.

26 *Pushkin, some 12 miles south of St. Petersburg, was known as Tsarskoe Selo (Czar's Village). Peter the Great gave his wife, Catherine I, a vast estate here on which their daughter Elizabeth subsequently built a palace, known as the Catherine Palace or simply Tsarskoe Selo. Its right wing incorporates an imperial church with domes in unmistakable Russian Baroque style, masterfully interpreted by the great Italian architect, Bartolomeo Rastrelli.*

The collections of the Hermitage are fabulous, and nearly infinite, and the terms are used advisedly (it contains at least 2.5 million masterpieces). Proceeding through the streets describing palaces and monuments in the copious order in which they are encountered would force us to fill the thousand or so pages that St. Petersburg demands for a minimum acceptable description. And so here we are, already beyond the church of St. Isaac on Theater Square: the largest theater, the Mariinsky, is the place where Glinka, Tchaikovsky, Mussorgsky, Rimsky-Korsakov, Glazunov, and Prokofiev first presented their works, to name just the most important composers; then comes the Conservatory, the church of St. Nicholas, the Synagogue, the arch of New Holland.

Close to St. Petersburg is Peterhof, with its great park, where the nearly 2000 sprays of 142 fountains jet skyward in an expression of the joy of life. In the middle of the park is the huge Peterhof palace designed by Rastrelli. The work of the great Italian architect can be found in another enchanting little town sixteen miles away from St. Petersburg, at Tsarskoje Selo is the great Catherine Palace, (often called simply Tsarskoje Selo), with its facade about a 1000 ft in length.

At this point we may choose to board the famous "Red Arrow" train and turn immediately to Moscow for a sharp contrast; this is the city built at the orders of the prince of Suzdal, Yurij Dolguruki, who built a little Kremlin there in 1156, later to become the building that we think of when we say "the Kremlin." A few wealthy merchants moved to the new town built on the Moscow (or Moskva) river. Within a few years, the city had grown in importance, to the point that Ivan III (1462-1505), after unifying the principalities of northern Russia, had himself proclaimed "Grand Duke of Moscow and All the Russias," and began to endow his Kremlin with churches and cathedrals. The first to be built was the Church of the Dormition of the Mother of God, built between 1475 and 1479 by Fioravanti. The Cathedral of the Annunciation followed (built between 1484 and 1489), and now possesses one of the most priceless iconostasis on earth, due to the work of Theophanes the Greek and Andrei Rublev. These two churches were soon joined by the Cathedral of the Archangel Michael (built between 1505 and 1508), where the mortal remains of all of the czars lie in neat rows of coffins. Other imperial churches within the Kremlin express their lavish and precious existence with their golden domes, rising over the roofs of the splendid buildings surrounding them. Ivan IV (1533-84), who had himself proclaimed czar in 1556, later having himself crowned emperor, built on the square facing the Kremlin the cathedral of St. Basil, in order to celebrate his victory over the Tatars at Kazan.

A second "kremlin" defending Moscow is the set of six fortified monasteries located to the south of the city, of which only one architectural treasure survives, the New Monastery of the Virgin, dating from 1524.

27 top Taken at Petrodvorets, a few miles from St.Petersburg, this picture shows one of the hundred fountains in the gardens of the Grand Palace, built by Peter the Great as a summer residence between 1714 and 1725.

27 bottom The Palace at Petrodvorets, with its seemingly interminable façade, has two gardens: a higher one at the main entrance, and a lower one at the rear, overlooking the Baltic Sea. Taking advantage of the seaward incline of the land and of the sea water itself, an intricate system supplies water to spectacular fountains and cascades.

28-29 The fountain in the former State Universal Store (better known as GUM) flows at the center of the famous building in Red Square, Moscow. The perfectly maintained structure reflects the elegant architecture of the late nineteenth century. Today Russia's oldest and largest department store looks drastically different as a result of the economic changes of recent years, and the former GUM now rivals Europe's finest stores. Decorated with the blue, white and red flag of the new Russia and packed with consumers, the huge shop sells articles of every kind.

The church, dedicated to the Dormition of the Mother of God, is adorned by one of the most glittering and original iconostases in all of Russia. If the Kremlin is the symbol of Russia, the Spasskaja Tower (1491), or of the Savior, is the symbol of the Kremlin, serving as its main gate. Outside of it is the new and old Moscow of the 18th, 19th, and 20th centuries, from the Museum of Russian History, built in handsome red brick, which constitutes the left-hand side of Red Square, to the long building of the Universal Department Stores (GUM), directly across from the Kremlin, wandering on through the city, after passing the ruins of the ancient walls of the Chinese City, one reaches the Neoclassical building of the Bolshoi, the Great Theater, which has its counterpart across the way: the Little Theater, with very interesting programs.

The theaters of Moscow are always worth all of the time that the visitor wishes to dedicate to them. Setting out from the Manège Square, one can walk along all of the Tverskaja Road, until recently Gorky Street, which is Moscow's rough equivalent of Nevsky Prospect.

After passing the Riding Academy heading in the other direction, one encounters the National Library, and farther along, the large and elegant Pushkin Museum, second only to the Hermitage, well known for its lavish collection of French Impressionists. Continuing along, one goes past the Moskva river and one reaches the Tretyakov Gallery, which houses the most splendid collection of Russian painting and the finest icons on earth (suffice it to mention the Virgin by Vladimir, the Trinity by Rublev, the Icons of Dionisi, as well as the finest icons of the schools of Pskov, Novgorod, Kiev, and Moscow). Beyond this, on the Sparrows Hills, from atop which Napoleon admired Moscow as it burned, fired by its own people, stands the skyscraper of the Lomonosov University, which houses 24,000 students, and has 45,000 rooms. Alongside its ancient and modern buildings, Moscow's true treasures are the immense parks and gardens, some of them built up and others left in a natural state of nature (Gorki, Ostankino, Izmaylovo, the Botanical Garden, Sokol'niki, Izmaylovo, to mention only the most important), each of them with its special character.

One could go on to describe the beauty of a great many other cities, towns, and villages: one cannot understand Russia with the mind, one cannot measure it by ordinary standards: Russia has a structure all its own, and one can do no more than tour it with an open heart. Even if one is captured by the celestial beauty of its enchantments, one will repeat the words of Sergei Aleksandrovich Esenin: "I have no need of Paradise, just give me my country."

Moscow the Eternal

30 top *Two symbolic presences characterize this shot of Moscow: a powerful, massive, Stalinist-Gothic palace and the glass pyramid that brings light to the underground subway station. Soviet Moscow and the new Moscow, oriented toward the future of technology, are today committed to coexistence.*

30 bottom *At the rear of the Kremlin, washed by the waters of the Moskva, we catch a glimpse of the high walls surrounding the most celebrated fortified enclosure in Russia. The country's first kremlin was built at Novgorod in 1044; Moscow's came three centuries later.*

31 *The Cathedral of St. Basil is the very symbol of Moscow and perhaps even of all Russia. Nobody would challenge its role as the country's most representative monument. With its onion-shaped domes it is known the world over, as much and even more than Westminster Abbey in London or the Louvre in Paris. In terms of celebrity, St. Mark's Basilica in Venice is perhaps its only rival.*

32-33 *The big GUM department store was built at the end of the 1800s. Long considered the Soviet answer to capitalist consumerism, it today holds an enormous mall in which it is possible to find a wide variety of food, clothing, and furnishings. The building's façade designed by the Russian architect Alexander Pomerantser is about 820 ft long.*

Magical buildings

34   *Here two splendid Moscow buildings stand practically face to face: the Spasskaya (Savior's) Gate Tower, in the central façade of the Kremlin, leading to Red Square, vies – in height at least-with the central dome of St. Basil's Cathedral.*

35 top   *At night three magical buildings that are the crowning glory of Red Square appear in their fairy-tale attire: left, the huge Kremlin fortress of Russia's czars; right, in the distance, blurred by an incantatory mist, the State Historical Museum; center-stage, as though set on a revolving platform, St. Basil's Cathedral, built to commemorate Russia's victory over the Tatars.*

35 center   *This panoramic view of the Kremlin by night gives flight to our imagination. Within its walls the powers-that-be are, perhaps, sleeping the sleep of the just. In its cathedrals, the saints of icons, Archangel Michael and the Madonna of all the Russias are keeping their loving watch over the Russian people.*

35 bottom   *The white bell tower of Ivan the Great was completed by Czsar Boris Godunov in 1600. In 1813 it was destroyed at the hands of Napoleon and his French troops (who believed the domes of the bell tower and churches to be made of solid gold!). It was later rebuilt, to a height of 272 ft. Comprised of four octagonal storeys plus a fifth round one, it is covered by a gilded dome 33 ft in diameter, surmounted by a 52 ft gold cross.*

36-37   *The statue of Marshal Georgi Zhukov sits in Revolyutsii Square, opposite the building containing the State Museum of History. Zhukov was a Second-World War hero and managed to stop Hitler at the gates of Moscow.*

38-39   *From a boat on the Moskva you get a superb view of the Presidential Palace, especially beneath the sun's dazzling rays. The new tricolor flag of the Russian Federated Republic is not hanging from the flagpole, so the President is not at home.*

40 top *The Cathedral of the Annunciation (Blagovesh-chensky Sobor) is an authentic gem. It was first built of wood by Andrei II, relative of Alexander Nevsky. Although subsequently burned, it was rebuilt in 1554 by Ivan the Terrible, and underwent extensive and definitive restoration in 1863-67. The golden domes of its nine chapels are instantly recognizable from the exterior.*

40 bottom *Rising over the Kremlin walls are the gilt roofs and domes of the Cathedral of the Annunciation, built on the highest point of the imperial fortress, so as to more effectively set off its golden profile against the backdrop of the sky.*

41 top left The Kremlin Church of the Deposition of the Sacred Vestment dates back to 1484-85. Like the Cathedral of the Annunciation it was constructed by master builders from Pskov, one of the first Russian towns where, in the early Middle Ages, buildings were already made of stone.

41 top right The bell tower of Ivan the Great was completed under Boris Godunov in 1600. Burned down, it was last rebuilt in 1812 following its destruction by the French. The bells – thirty-four of varying sizes – are reached after ascending 450 steep steps. The largest bell, a gift from Czar Alexander I, is rung only twice a year, at Christmas and Easter.

41 bottom This "bunch" of golden domes could almost be souls gathering to prepare for the journey heavenward; or precious air-balloons perhaps, carrying the prayers of men, to lay them at the feet of the Almighty.

42-43 The interior of a Kremlin cathedral is perhaps already a reflection of Paradise, of the other world beyond the Golden Gates.

44 and 45 *Once home of the Czars, the Great Kremlin Palace – 397 ft long, and 420 ft wide – is still the residence of Russia's leaders. It incorporates many other splendid buildings and rooms: the Vladimir Room, St. George's Room, the Golden Room and the old Terem Palace, its icons further enhanced by the predominating red of its décor.*

46 left *The Armory has always been used as the Kremlin's museum. Few people are aware that the czars' most precious treasures always remained in this Moscow building – even when, in the 18th century, Peter the Great moved Russia's capital and the czars'* place of residence to St. Petersburg. Among the exhibits is one of the famous eggs created for the Romanov family in the jewelry workshops of Carl Fabergé. These elaborate works of fantasy exemplify outstanding craft skills and miniaturization techniques.

46 right *Another gem of enormous worth that is both an exquisite work of art and a piece of imperial history: one of tens of thousands of items displayed in the Armory (Oruzheynaya) Palace, now the Kremlin State Museum.*

47

47 *Instead of a ride in a carriage, you can take an interesting stroll among the czars' richly ornamented State carriages, on show in the Armory Palace.*

Decorative arts and ballet

48-49 *On stage at the Bolshoi – the high temple of ballet – Ekaterina Maksimova and Vladimir Vasilyev dance the dramatic finale of Valeri Gavrilin's ballet,* Anyuta. *The theater's renown as the home of ballet is linked to the arrival, in 1812, of the danseur noble Adam Pavlovich Glushkovski and – even more so – to the memorable production of Adolphe Adam's* Giselle *in 1843.*

49 top *The Bolshoi Theater was established in 1780 with the name of Petrovksy Theater, after the street where it stood. It burned down in 1805 and reconstructed in 1824. This building too was destroyed by fire, in 1853. It was again rebuilt with improved acoustics. When a smaller auditorium was opened in 1919, Petrovsky automatically become the "Big Theater," the Bolshoi.*

49 bottom left *A performance of* Tosca *is in progress at the Bolshoi. Since the theater's earliest days a very special relationship developed between the Bolshoi and the Italian artistes who, in the 19th century, directed its productions. This situation was not accepted by Russian performers and composers, led by Peter Ilyich Tchaikovsky. Yet this rivalry bore significant fruits: the great Russian composer subsequently created ballets and music celebrated everywhere.*

49 bottom right *This photo shows another scene from* Anyuta *with Maksimova in the foreground. Born in Moscow in 1939, she was still a pupil at the theater's Ballet School when she made her Bolshoi debut as Masha in Tchaikovsky's* Nutcracker. *Under the direction of Galina Ulanova, she has interpreted all the most prestigious roles of the Bolshoi repertoire. Her exceptional qualities as a dancer have made her a leading contemporary prima ballerina.*

Quiet and chaos in the heart of Moscow

50 top *Numerous historic bridges cross Moscow River. The one shown in the photo is one of the most famous: it is Bolshoi Kamenny Most, which links the south side of the city with the Kremlin.*

50 center *After having wandered around Moscow, a quick break on a park bench can revive or relax. Muscovites love to stroll among the trees and in the open green spaces offered by the capital.*

50 bottom *Muscovites spend many pleasant hours in the city parks. The most famous is Gorky Park, but there are many, like Aleksandrovsky Park shown in the photo, packed on weekends and holidays, both in summer and winter.*

50-51 *The road to St. Petersburg leaves from Tverskaya Ulitsa. An important artery for the city, tramlines and lanes for cars weave along it, whereas numerous restaurants and some of Moscow's most elegant shops line its sidewalks.*

52 *The photos, from top to bottom, show Hard Rock Café, American Café, and one of the many McDonald's that are multiplying throughout the Russian capital. In Moscow, more than in the rest of the country, economic development has passed through a vague commercial opening to the West, the effects of which are highly visible in the signs of bars and restaurants. Increasingly, these use the English, as do the Latin alphabet in advertisements, which proliferate on city walls. America, once the Cold War enemy, is today a model.*

52-53 *Gastronom No. 1 in Moscow is not just a mere bureaucratic numeration. The luxurious shop on Tverskaya Street (also called Gorky Street) is "No. 1" in the full sense of the word, since it is the well-known Eliseevsky Magazin, the "Shop of Eliseev," the most famous, high-class, elegant food shop in Moscow, open since the beginning of the 20th century.*

55 top *Forever the hub of inner Moscow, Arbat Street is the heart of a modern consumer focused Russia. On this street, one takes walks, makes purchases, and shows off new clothes.*

55 center *A giant billboard featuring a luxurious Asian automobile sits on the building containing the headquarters of MTS, a cellular phone company. Two symbols of Moscow of the third millennium are united in a single image.*

55 bottom *Near what once was a monument to totalitarianism and terror, Lubyanka Prison, today stand the large shopping centers representative of neo-consumerism.*

56-57 *Old buildings sporting paradigms for new lifestyles on their walls: Moscow is still a crossroads of contradictions, where traces of the past exist alongside a great push toward the future.*

The big chill

58-59 *If Arbat Street is the most famous street in Moscow, New Arbat St. is the incarnation of the urban gigantism typical of the post-war years. In the photo, one of the twin skyscrapers built in the 1960s rises in the background of spectacular illuminated signs.*

РЕСТОРАН
ТРОПИКАНА

КАЗИНО

КУЛЬТУРНО-РАЗВЛЕКАТЕЛЬНЫЙ

59 *A mix of styles and a tangled center of neo-capitalist stimuli, New Arbat St. is dominated by flashy tastes. The "new Arbat" area was created in the 1970s by flattening an entire neighborhood, which happened to contain dozens of streets, a monastery, and several churches. Within the scope of the same urban development program, four twin skyscrapers were built, in which the headquarters of some important government ministries were established.*

60-61 *The nouveau riche of modern Russia – oil barons, mineral industrialists, and corporate bosses in the telecommunications field – are the tip of the iceberg of an upper class determined to spend and be seen. In present-day Moscow, there is plenty of room for the status symbols most disdained during the Soviet era, such as fast Italian sport cars.*

62 Interior galleries of GUM are always full of Muscovites, who find shelter there during winter strolls or when are looking for any kind of commercial goods. The store's architectural structure has remained virtually unchanged since its foundation.

63 Great brands and great names in fashion in an atmosphere that, having preserved its 19th-century style, is distinguished by an elegant dignity: the great Muscovite department store has changed remarkably with respect to the not-so-distant years in which endless lines wound past half-empty shelves and products of dubious quality.

64-65 Domes, windows, and fountains characterize the large Okhotnyi Ryad shopping mall at the far north side of Red Square.

66-67 With 2700 ft. of façade, the GUM department store has looked onto Red Square for over a century.

Splendid Testimonials
of Bygone Days

68 top *The spacious square at Pavlovsk is enclosed by a semi-circular gallery and colonnade, to a design by Vincenzo Brenna.*

68 bottom *Neglected by Czar Paul, who preferred the summer residence at Gatchina, the Czarina Maria Fyodorovna took the Pavlovsk palace in hand. She commissioned elegant new buildings and other structures in the large park and lavishly furnished the interiors with fine furniture, Gobelin tapestries, paintings, decorative majolica and exquisite tablewares.*

69 *At a distance of 12 miles from St. Petersburg lies Pavlovsk. The site of this city was a gift from Catherine II to her newly-born son and heir, Paul, subsequently father of Czar Alexander I. The palace built here – designed by the Scottish architect Charles Cameron, in Roman style – was completed by Vincenzo Brenna with the collaboration of Quarenghi and Rossi. A somewhat unusual statue of Paul dressed in Prussian military uniform stands at the center of the main courtyard.*

St. Petersburg, jewel of the Baltic

70 *The dome of the Admiralty, topped by an octagonal spire tiled with gilded plates, rises at the intersection of Nevsky prospect, Gorokhovayia Street, and Voznesensky prospect and dominates the skyline of St. Petersburg. The Admiralty was built between 1806 and 1823 on the banks of the Neva River according to designs by the architect Andrei Zakharov, in what passed into history as the "imperial Russian style."*

71 top *Palace Square (Dvortzovaya Ploshchad) offers a wide assortment of architectural styles. On the northern side stands the Winter Palace; opposite, Rossi's General Staff building, commissioned by Alexander I; continuing eastwards, the Palace of the Regiment of the Guard. In the center of the square the Alexander Column rises to a height of 157 ft. Together with the triumphal arch at the side of the General Staff Building, it commemorates Alexander's victory over Napoleon.*

71 center *A panoramic view of St. Petersburg, a city which has made evident Russia's desire to bridge its "technological" distance from the West by inviting prominent Westerners to participate in its development: in the 18th and 19th centuries, primarily artists and architects; in the coming years of the 20th and 21st centuries, experts in advanced areas of industrial technology.*

71 bottom *The cruiser* Aurora, *anchored near the bridge over the Neva, had the symbolic task of firing the first cannon of the great Russian Revolution of 1917, as a signal to the Bolsheviks to attack the Winter Palace.*

72-73 *The Dvortcoviy Most (Palace Bridge) connects mainland St. Petersburg to the Strelka, the easternmost point of Vasilevsky Island. Nighttime lighting increases the charm of the Admiralty and the Neva River. The 19th-century rostral columns can be spotted on the far right of the photo.*

75 top *In its original form, the Winter Palace commissioned by Peter the Great was an unpretentious – but later enlarged – two-storey building. It was here that Peter died, in 1725. Rastrelli worked on further extending the palace and restructuring its interiors – the throne room and central staircase were built to his plans – completing the palace in 1762.*

75 center *Yet another fire destroyed the palace in 1837 and it was subsequently recreated according to the original plans. Even all the furniture was re-made, in Neo-Classical style.*

75 bottom *As a tribute to Russia's governors, the vast room used for balls and other court functions is decorated with their coats of arms – hence its name, the Coats of Arms Room.*

76-77 *The splendid staircase – known as the Ambassadors' Staircase – also bears Rastrelli's name. Destroyed in the fire of 1837, it was rebuilt with only minor changes, attributable to the different building materials used. These stairs led to the reception rooms on the first floor of the Winter Palace; the imperial family also used the staircase when going to State religious services.*

Russia's own Versailles

78-79 *This picture is of Peterhof, some 19 miles from St. Petersburg. Dominating the park on its upper terrace is a large statue of Neptune. The history of this statue and its fountain is a rather curious tale: the work of two 17th-century German sculptors, commissioned for the city of Nurenberg, it was never installed due to the unavailability of water inadequate volume and at sufficient pressure.*

79 *The single dome of the church that is incorporated into Peterhof is yet another work of the prolific Rastrelli, and dates to 1751.*

80-81 *This photo shows the Grand Cascade and the Fountain of Samson in its full splendor. On the lower terrace of the gardens surrounding Peterhof are no fewer than 144 fountains and three cascades, their decorative flows and jets of water creating wonderful displays for visitors.*

83 top *An unusual and elegantly contoured dome crowns the Peterhof church, which stands on the east side of this huge building (its main block alone is 902 ft long). At the far end of the west side is the two-headed eagle.*

83 center *The Blue Room was kept in readiness for guests, its table set with thirty places. The dinner service on display is dated 1850 and was made in Russia.*

83 bottom *The interiors of Peterhof are exuberant examples of the finest Russian Baroque. Abundant use is made of gold and stucco, in keeping with the taste and style of Rastrelli who designed most of the rooms in this building – among them the Oak Cabinet created for Peter the Great in 1718-1720 – all richly endowed with silks, intarsia, mirrors, Chinese vases, tapestries, paintings and porcelain wares.*

The treasure houses of Russian artworks

84 top *This palace, known for its blu-and-white façade, was designed by Rastrelli for Elizabeth I (1741-62), who named it the Catherine Palace in honour of her mother, Czarina Catherine I (1725-27), second wife of Peter the Great. It stands on land that Peter gave to Catherine, close to the village of Tsarskoe selo, near the Baltic. The name did not derive from the word "czar" meaning emperor, but from a disotrted adaptation of the Finnish name of the locality which was Saari (high) Muis (farm), fisr called Saarskoye Selo, the Sarskoye Selo and eventually Tsarskoye Selo, meaning "Village of the czar." In the 1930s, Tsarskoe Selo was renamed Pushkin (the poet studied at the Imperial Lyceum at Tsarskoe Selo, but was recently retaken its traditional name.*

84 center *The Palace of Catherine (often referred to as Tsarskoe Selo) is an important art museum of European standing: of the 130 paintings in the Picture Gallery, 114 are notable Flemish, Italian and French works of the 17th and 18th centuries.*

84 bottom *The Russian Museum in St. Petersburg, is second only the Tretyakov in Moscow as a showcase of Russian art. It is housed in the Mikhailovsky Palace, designed by Carlo Rossi in 1819, for Alexander I's younger brother Mikhail. With its vast collections of paintings (as many as 300,000), the museum offers an overview of Russian art from its origins to the early 20th century.*

84-85 *The Great Hall at Tsarskoye Selo measures 157 by 59 ft and is certainly Rastrelli's boldest creation. The glitter of gold and ornamentation is brilliantly illuminated by no fewer than 696 candles.*

Masterpieces inspired by faith

86 top left *The Smolny Institute, designed by Giacomo Quarenghi (1808), was frequented by young aristocrats of 19th-century St. Petersburg. It was named after the nearby convent which in turn obtained its name from a workshop where resin and pitch* (smola *in Russian*) *were produced. The building was used by Lenin for Bolshevik meetings during the Revolution of 1917.*

86 top right *In the Smolny Convent complex the Cathedral of the Resurrection shows the unmistakable hand of Rastrelli and his variant of Russian Baroque, here exemplified by depth of color (blue) and solid monumentality. Founded in 1748 by Czarina Elizabeth 1 who intended to retire here in old age, the convent was not completed until late 18th century, by Catherine II.*

86 bottom *The Cathedral of the Our Lady of Kazan was commissioned by Czar Paul II and built on the model of St. Peter's Basilica in Rome; its sculptured doors are instead copies of those of the Baptistery of St. John Lateran in Florence, except that here the stories depicted are of the Russian saints Andrei, Vladimir and Alexander Nevksy. An imposing semicircular colonnade with 43-ft-high pillars completes the ensemble. With its dome the cathedral rises to 230 ft in height.*

87 *The large Cathedral of Christ Our Savior (Khram Khrista Spasitelya) stands on the spot where a previous church of the same name was destroyed by Stalin to make way for a giant monument to Lenin, designed but never actually built. The church was inaugurated in 1997 on the occasion of the 850th anniversary of the foundation of Moscow.*

89 left *Among the buildings of the Trinity-St. Sergius monastery complex in Zagorsk, the Cathedral of the Assumption (1559-85) with its brilliant blue and golden domes is instantly recognizable. It was built at the time of Ivan the Terrible, on the highest point within the monastery walls, following the model of the Kremlin church. Sergius of Radonezh was the son of a nobleman from Rostov; after he became a monk, his wanderings eventually brought him to Zagorsk, around the year 1338. With the aid of a few fellow monks he built a wooden church, laying the foundations for the monastery which soon became renowned for its ancient manuscripts and icon-painting school.*

89 right *Ordinary Russians whose faith is spontaneous and boundless, often give vent to their devotion with shows of great enthusiasm, even exaltation. In the churches of the West religious faith is no longer expressed with external manifestations of joy and fervor, as it still is the case in Russia.*

90-91 *The iconostasis the Cathedral of the Assumption in Vladimir has a beauty that defies description. The figures and scenes it depicts are not positioned at random but follow precise doctrinal dictates. For instance, the image of Christ is always to the right of the golden doors, while that of Mary his Mother is to the left; the top part contains anecdotal references or scenes from the life of the saint to whom the church is dedicated.*

91 top left *Originally built in 1158-64 the Golden Gates of the city of Vladimir were reconstructed in the 17th/18th centuries. Adjoining them is the contemporary Cathedral of the Assumption, in white stone. The fortress town of Vladimir was founded by Vladimir II Monomakh in 1116. It was chosen as the permanent home of Prince Andrei Yurievich who, from 1169 onwards, enlarged and embellished it, incorporating nearby Bogolyubovo. Sacked and devastated by the Tatars in 1238, it was subsequently rebuilt, but a century later church and temporal authority were transferred to the principality of Moscow.*

91 top right *The Cathedral of the Assumption (Uspensky), in Vladimir, contains precious frescoes by Rublev from 1405. Andrei Rublev (1370-1427) founded the Muscovite school of painting and was the greatest Russian painter in history. While a monk at Trinity-St. Sergius in Zagorsk, he painted* The Trinity, *which is considered to be his masterpiece, although his icons of the Savior, Archangel Michael, and the Apostle Paul are no less important.*

91 bottom *The Cathedral of the Assumption in Vladimir is one of the most splendid of the city's twenty-eight churches. Built by Prince Andrei in the 12th century, it was later destroyed by Tatars along with the rest of the city. But in 1432 an even finer church was built on the site: for many years it was regarded as the most important cathedral in Russia, and the mortal remains of Russia's most noteworthy princes – from Vladimir to the Great Princes of Moscow – were buried here.*

92 *Rostov Veliki is one of the cities of Russia's Golden Ring and it was first mentioned in chronicles in 862. In the 10th century it became capital of the principality of Rostov-Suzdal. Like many other Russian principalities it came under Moscow's control, in 1474. Its imposing walls enclose a plethora of architectural treasures: the Cathedral of the Assumption, the bell tower with its thirteen columns, the church of St. John the Theologian, three ancient monasteries incorporating equally old churches and the round towers of the kremlin, a sight not easily forgotten.*

92-93 *The kremlin in Rostov Veliki (Rostov the Great) is just one of its the magnificent buildings. The city's churches have an unusual feature: frescoed walls and a stone altar in the place of the traditional iconostasis. An example can be seen in the Cathedral of the Savior in the Shade. The frescoes are the work of the Rostov school established by the Orthodox pope Timothy as well as of Dmitri Stepanov and Ivan and Fyodor Karpov.*

94 top left *The exquisite iconostasis of the Cathedral of St. John the Baptist, or Precursor, as he is also called by the Orthodox Church. The cathedral was built in just sixteen years, from 1671 to 1687. St. John the Precursor is also very popular in Russia (boys are named Ivan after this saint, not after St. John the Evangelist), since he is considered a model of the constant penitence that Russian people of faith aspire to.*

94 bottom left *This picture shows a precious icon of St. Nicholas, in Yaroslavl. St. Nicholas is the patron saint of peasants and harvests; he is always depicted with his stole crossed on his chest, the Gospel in his left hand and his right hand held up in blessing.*

94 right *The Church of the Prophet Elijah was built in 1646-50. According to scholars, the special veneration shown for this saint by Russians (and Slavs generally) is to be attributed to his confusion with the god of storms since, on account of the story told in the Bible, he is thought to be connected with thunderbolts.*

95 *Yaroslavl was founded in the early 11th century by Yaroslav the Wise. The city has many fine historic buildings, in particular the Transfiguration of Our Savior Monastery complex; set against its rear walls, built in the 16th-17th centuries, is a most unusual church of this name, triangular in shape. The church of the Prophet Elijah is renowned for its outstanding frescoes and iconostasis.*

97 top *The Cathedral of the Transfiguration in the city of Suzdal was built in 1564; most of its frescoes are the work of G.Nikitin, a great 17th-century icon painter. After a period of unification with the principality of Rostov, in 1392 Suzdal became one of the first cities to be annexed by the princes of Moscow. Once its political importance had waned, it became one of the country's leading religious centers.*

97 center *The kremlin of Suzdal dates back to the 12th century; its celebrated Golden Gates were added in 1688. Within its walls stands the Cathedral of the Birth of the Mother of God: built in 1222, it is one of Russia's oldest stone churches, embellished with magnificent frescoes in the 12th, 15th and 17th centuries. The blue-green color of its domes is quite unique. No tour of Russia's Golden Ring would be complete without a visit to Suzdal.*

97 bottom *Novgorod, built along both banks of the Volkhov river, was first mentioned in chronicles as early as 859. By the 10th century it was the second most important cultural and trading center in Russia. From 1136 to 1478 it was a self-governing republic. On the left bank of the river stands the kremlin, built in 1044 and surrounded by imposing walls and towers (rebuilt 1484-1490). The finest building is undoubtedly the Cathedral of St. Sofia, patron saint of the city, ornamented with splendid icons of the Novgorod school, considered by many to be the most important to have existed in Russia.*

Boundless Wide-open Spaces

98 top *The warm shades of autumn bring a colorful note to the right bank of Lake Baikal, in southern Siberia, in the Irkutsk region of the Buryat republic. Baikal is the deepest body of water on Earth (maximum depth 5315 ft) and has 27 islands, 5 of them inhabitable year round. Into Lake Baikal flow 336 rivers, of which the largest are the Angara and Selenga. In summer the water temperature is around 12° C but reaches 20° C in the offshore shallows, making the lake the most popular holiday destination in Siberia and Central Russia.*

98 bottom *Vyborg, the ancient Finnish town of Viipuri, in the Karelia region, was founded as a fortress by the Swedes in 1293. After the Russians defeated the Swedes and took over the town, the fortress of Vyborg came to be used as a much-feared prison. Among the illustrious figures imprisoned there over the centuries were some of Decembrists, the officers who – in the name of freedom of opinion – rebelled against the czar in 1825. Finland has always claimed sovereignty over Vyborg, and its ownership has depended on the two nations' alternating fortunes in war. Since 1944, it has been part of the district of Leningrad, which is governed by the city of St. Petersburg.*

99 *This aerial photo – taken in the Kamchatka Peninsula – 120° longitude East of the town of Vyborg, on the Gulf of Finland – shows the abundant vegetation in the Kronos National Park, a nature reserve. Prominent in the background is the perfect profile of the peak of the volcano of the same name.*

The grainlands of Russia

100 *This farmer lives in the Vologda region, between Moscow and Novgorod. When the USSR ceased to exist (on December 21, 1991), a new system of land distribution was introduced, based on private ownership. This has inevitably created huge problems in the agricultural sector, previously centrally controlled and based on collective and state farms (kolkhoz and sovkhoz, respectively). At the present time average productivity of independent Russian farmers is thought to be only one third of that in more developed agricultural nations.*

101 top *Looking at this sea of golden corn, we can only hope that Russia succeeds in speeding up the pace of mechanization of its agricultural sector, to enable it to satisfy its home market's incredibly high demand for flour and bread.*

101 bottom *Harvesting wheat on the vast farmlands of Russia calls for powerful machinery and greater automation.*

Age-old traditions and lifestyles

102 *Sergiev Posad is an excellent example of an old "double-sided" village. Wooden houses flank the two sides of the street at an incredibly short distance from those opposite, and oblivious to the evident risk of fire. At one time exogamy was practiced in Russian villages (marrying a person from one's own village was not allowed): all the people living in one row of houses considered themselves as relatives and were obliged to look for a suitable spouse "on the opposite side of the street" (or bridge, if a stream flowed through the village).*

102-103 *This picture is of an* izba *in Sergiev Posad (Zagorsk). The Russian* izba *(its name is derived from the Old High German word "stuba," meaning heated room) was originally made entirely of wood, without masonry foundations and with overhanging beams at the four corners. The basement is used as a storage place for provisions, the ground floor as a workshop or for other storage needs while upstairs is the heated living area.*

104 top *Few peoples whose livelihood comes from the land are as skillful at woodwork as the Russians, who can work wonders even with a simple axe (a topor). This craftsman has used his manual and creative skills to add a decorative note to the windows of an izba in Sergiev Posad (Zagorsk). And a closer look at his work suggests a possible link between this ornamental art and the much grander Russian Baroque style.*

104 bottom *Siberian fishermen don't lose heart if the river freezes: there's always some way of getting fish to bite and the cold of Krasnoyarsk helps sharpen a fisherman's wits. Founded as a fort in 1628 when the gradual conquest of Siberia was in progress, Krasnoyarsk became an important port on the River Yenisei, especially after gold was discovered in the region. As a consequence of the notable growth of the city, its population is now close to one million.*

104-105 *The museum-ship "Sv.Nikolai" is the vessel on which Lenin crossed the Yenisei, in 1897, when travelling from Krasnoyarsk to the village of Shushenskoye, where he spent three years in exile.*

106-107 *The Yenisei, Siberia's longest river, has two parts: the Great Yenisei, called Biy-Khem in Evenk, and the Small Yenisei or Ka-Khem. Together they cut Siberia practically in two, from the Sayan mountains in Northern Mongolia to the Kara Sea on the margins of the Arctic* *Ocean. The total length of the river is more than 2000 miles, with a maximum width of 12 miles. The Yenisei is the greatest drainage basin in Russia. There are major hydroelectric power facilities along its length and in summer months its shores attract crowds of bathers.*

108 *The Caucasian peoples are well-known for their pride and their strong attachment to tradition. These qualities have played a major part in keeping the various ethnic groups separate for thousands of years; they also help explain their longing for autonomy.*

109 top *The Russian Federation has many different nationalities. Prominent among them are the Caucasian peoples, comprised of numerous ethnic groups with different languages and customs but often common origins. Besides the Armenians, perhaps the foremost Caucasian people are the Georgians. But also have strong identities, among them other ethnic groups: Chechens, Ingush, Kabardins, Circassians, and Osetians. They all live in mainly mountainous regions and their traditional economy is based on cattle and sheep herding. Excellent horsemen and warriors, the peoples of the Caucasus still attribute importance to age-old rites and customs.*

109 bottom *The Caucasus spans the isthmus that separates the Black Sea and Sea of Asov from the Caspian Sea, a region considered one of the oldest settled areas on Earth. Several Caucasian mountains are over 16,400 ft high: these include Mt.Elbrus (18,510 ft) and Mt.Kazbek (16,512 ft).*

110-111 *The people of Siberia call the huge Lake Baikal "holy." Its name comes from the Turkiic-Siberian* bai *meaning rich, and* koel, *lake. Not only does the fish-rich lake provide a livelihood for the populations that live around it; it also helps make the climate much milder than in the surounding territory. And each evening, the sunset reflected in its moving waters is pure spectacle.*

112-113 *The peace and quiet that descends on a Siberian village as nightfall approaches is almost tangible. People who have witnessed for themselves the clear skies over the taiga say they have seen nothing similar anywhere else on Earth.*

114 *The word taiga is used when referring to Siberia's vast stretches of coniferous forests, beneath the tundra zone. But in Turkic-Siberian tai-ga means "rocky mountain" and the typical taiga vegetation is in fact often interspersed with rocky outcrops. Evidence of this can be seen in the southernmost part of Yakutia, along the banks of a tributary of the River Lena.*

115 *Dominating the landscape in southern Siberia, to the north of China and Mongolia, are the Altai mountains. The Ob, Irtysh and Yenisei rivers – the three main rivers of Siberia, among the largest in the world – have their sources in this mountain range.*

116 *For the Yukaghirs a sleigh is much more than their sole means of transport. When they set up camp, it also serves as worktop, cradle and bed.*

116-117 *The most ancient population of Siberia – the real Paleosiberians – are the Nivkh-Yukaghir peoples, whose customs and languages are unaffiliated to the many others of the immense Asian territories of Russia. They are essentially hunters and reindeer herdsmen, used to living in the severest of climates, with temperatures at the limit of human resistance. In prehistoric times Aleuts and possibly also Tungus-Mongol peoples crossed the Bering Strait to settle in North and South America.*

Last stop, Vladivostok

118-119 *Vladivostok Station marks the end of an interminable journey, one that train enthusiasts dream about... And it is curious to note that, in its architecture, the terminus resembles Kazan Station in Moscow, where the journey started. The very name of* *Vladivostok (it means "Rule the East") gives of an idea of its role as a city. It is one of the largest ports on the Pacific Ocean, and very close to Japan and Korea. Founded as a military outpost in 1860, Vladivostok now has a population of over 700,000.*

119 top *For many years Vladivostok was a "closed" city, a naval base where only sailors and their families lived. As such it was inaccessible to Russian travelers as well as to foreigners. At that time the Trans-Siberian Railway ended its journey in the city of Chita, in the Mongol-Buryat region.*

119 bottom *Russia's naval fleet is divided among the seas it controls. The Pacific Ocean fleet is based in Vladivostok, the Black Sea fleet in Odessa and the Baltic fleet in St. Petersburg. Considering both merchant and military shipping, in terms of tonnage and number of vessels, Russia's navy is the largest in the world.*

120-121 *This picture offers a view of the city and port of Vladivostok. There are many attractive localities in the vicinity and, they have become popular tourist destinations. Evening can be a beautiful time here, as the setting sun turns from red to pink on the distant Pacific horizon.*

122-123 *The bay of Vladivostok has numerous inlets where the water is crystal-clear and nature still unspoilt. In 1916 the huge Kedrovaya Pad nature reserve was established on the banks of the River Amur. In an area of almost 20,000 hectares assorted oceanic and Manchurian-Siberian flora flourish, as well as rare trees. The forest is inhabited by many different animal species, including leopards, tigers, spotted reindeer, Himalayan bears, and Ussuri rhinoceroses. Very rare species of birds are also seen here.*

119

125 top *In the reserve at the foot of Mt. Kronos animals live in freedom, in a protected environment. The milder climate of this area means there are plentiful supplies of grass, plants and also fish for the reserve's greediest bears.*

125 bottom *On the Pacific side of the peninsula the volcanoes soar to heights of over 9850 ft. The craters of the Avacha and Koryalsky volcanoes – still active beneath their perpetual snows – can be seen in this picture.*

124 *By air, the distance from Kedrovaya Pad to the Kamchatka reserve is relatively short. The scene that greets visitors is spectacular: an astounding landscape littered with the huge craters of volcanoes.*

126-127 *Lights shine from the windows of a ranger's house in the Mt. Kronos reserve: a point of reference for the many animal species that populate this stupendous, unspoilt natural environment at the very edge of Russia. When night is descending over Kamchatka, Moscow is waking up, about to add another day to Russia's long history.*

128 *Three young street vendors, in their sponsor's red jackets, sell beverages and snacks to tourists passing by the monument to Marshal Zhukov. An unimaginable image in the Russia of yesterday, it is common in today's Russia.*